MATT CHRISTOPHER

On the Court with...

Venus and Serena Williams

MATT CHRISTOPHER

On the Court with...

Venus and Serena Williams

Text by Glenn Stout

Little, Brown and Company

Boston   New York   London

First Edition

Matt Christopher™ is a trademark of Catherine M. Christopher.

Cover photograph by Elise Amendola /Associated Press

Library of Congress Cataloging-in-Publication Data

Stout, Glenn.
    On the court with . . . Venus and Serena Williams/text by Glenn
Stout.—1st ed.
        p. cm.
    ISBN 0-316-13814-2 (pb)
    1. Williams, Venus, 1980– — Juvenile literature.   2. Williams,
Serena, 1981– — Juvenile literature.   3. Tennis players — United
States — Biography — Juvenile literature.   4. African American
women tennis players — Biography — Juvenile literature.   I. Title: At
head of title: Matt Christopher.   II. Christopher, Matt.   III. Title.
GV994.A1 S86   2002
796.342'092'273
[B] — dc21   2001038452

10 9 8 7 6 5 4 3 2 1

COM-MO

Printed in the United States of America

Contents

Chapter One: 1980–1985   1
The Tennis Players

Chapter Two: 1985–1991   11
Potential Prodigy

Chapter Three: 1991–1994   24
Tennis School

Chapter Four: 1994   35
The Professional

Chapter Five: 1995–1997   46
Tourney Time

Chapter Six: 1998   55
Breaking Through

Chapter Seven: 1999   66
We Are Family

Chapter Eight: 1999   74
Slamming Sister

Chapter Nine: 1999–2000   87
Venus Rising

Chapter Ten: 2001   100
Onward and Upward?

Chapter One:
1980-1985

The Tennis Players

One warm summer morning in 1984, a father loaded his Volkswagen van for a special trip. He carefully placed seven milk crates full of tennis balls and several tennis rackets in the back of the van. Then he went back in the house and called for his four-year-old daughter. They were going to go somewhere special.

The little girl eagerly followed him. She loved going places with her father.

They drove from their modest Compton, California, home toward a nearby public park. They wound through the city streets, surrounded by depressing scenery. Compton, an inner-city community near Los Angeles, would be described by most people as a ghetto. The city is poor, and many residents of the mostly African-American and Hispanic

1

community struggle to make ends meet. The buildings and many homes are run-down. Crime and poverty are rampant. While most residents are hard-working and law-abiding citizens, many live day-to-day, with little thought of the future.

But the future was all the girl's father was thinking about. Several years before, he'd watched a women's tennis match on television. The winner, Virginia Ruzici, earned nearly thirty thousand dollars for winning the tournament. Richard Williams was impressed. Professional tennis players traveled the world, and the best made thousands of dollars playing one or two matches a day for three or four days every couple of weeks. Seeing that match had given him an idea.

Now it was time to test that idea. Williams wanted his daughter to become a tennis player. He pulled into a small parking lot adjacent to the park.

On the other side of a chain-link fence were several tennis courts, although no one was playing tennis on them. A few young men lingered on the sidelines, just hanging out. Glass from broken bottles glistened on the court, the surface of which was spray-painted with graffiti.

Williams helped his daughter from the van and retrieved the crates of balls, a broom, and two tennis rackets. He led his daughter through the gate to the court and had her stand to the side for a few moments while he swept the court free of glass.

Then he motioned for her to join him, put a racket in her hands, and showed her how to hold it. He grabbed a tennis ball, tossed it in the air, and gently used his racket to direct it toward his daughter. "Swing at the ball," he called out.

His little daughter giggled and tried to swing the racket. It was nearly as big as she was, and her momentum spun her almost completely around. She missed the ball, which bounced and rolled away.

For the next hour they stood in the hot sun, father and daughter, as Williams patiently began to teach his young daughter how to strike a tennis ball with a tennis racket. At first she struck the ball mostly by accident.

When the crates were empty, the two would gather up the loose balls, making a game of seeing who could get the most balls in the crate, and start over. The father would occasionally stop, place his hand around his daughter's on the racket, and show her how to sweep it through the air and strike the ball in the center of the racket's strings.

The young girl showed amazing patience for a four-year-old, and after an hour or so she began to make consistent contact with the ball. When the crate was empty again, the father held up the last ball. "Last one!" he called out.

"Last one," his daughter responded with a laugh. Then he gently knocked the ball toward her, and she swung.

Thwack! The ball made a distinctive sound as it struck the racket.

The father and daughter gathered up the tennis balls, loaded them back into the van, and returned home.

When they got out of the car, the man's other daughter, still several weeks shy of her third birthday, greeted them. She felt left out and was pouting. She hated being apart from her sister. The father explained to her that she'd soon be able to come along on the trips to the park.

The tennis careers of Venus and Serena Williams had begun.

Their father's dream has come true, for now the

Williams sisters are two of the biggest stars in women's tennis. They travel the world and make thousands of dollars playing tennis a few hours a day every couple of weeks. Endorsements earn each sister millions more.

Such riches were only a dream when Richard Williams was growing up in Shreveport, Louisiana. His parents were sharecroppers, farmers who worked a small plot of land for the landowner, supporting themselves by exchanging their crop for rent and food. It is a hard way to make a living. Sharecroppers are often far in debt to their landlord and have to work long hours just to keep up.

When he was a young boy, Richard often had to work in the field with his parents. As he grew up, he was determined to make a better life for his family.

Sports became one of Richard's few escapes from the rigors of working in the fields. He and his friends, the children of other sharecroppers, would spend what little free time they had playing sports like baseball, football, and basketball. But there were no organized youth leagues, and there was no time to play on school teams. Still, Richard was a good athlete, and he enjoyed playing.

When he was a young man, Richard moved around a lot and worked a variety of jobs. He met a young nurse named Oracene, whom everyone called Brandi. She had grown up in a middle-class family in Michigan. Despite their different backgrounds, the two soon fell in love, married, and started a family.

Their first daughter, Yetunde, was born in 1972. She was followed a year later by Isha, then five years later by Lyndrell. Venus was born on June 17, 1980, and Serena a little over a year later, on September 26, 1981.

The family moved around a lot, going back and forth across the country several times before finally settling in Compton. Brandi worried about raising the girls in such a rough place, but Richard believed his daughters would benefit from growing up in such an environment. He wanted them to learn to be strong.

While Brandi worked as a nurse, Richard ran a small security company. With some friends in the neighborhood, he also learned how to play tennis.

Before going to work in the morning, he would meet a group of friends to play at a city park. Richard had never played before. At first, he learned by watching, but he soon began to teach himself, studying books about the game and watching matches on television.

He couldn't help but notice that there were very few African Americans who played tennis, particularly professionally.

The game had evolved from a French game known as *paume,* which is similar to handball. Players eventually began using rackets to strike the ball, and it evolved into an indoor game known as "court tennis." Court tennis required an indoor court and was played mainly by royalty and other very wealthy people who could afford to build an indoor court.

In the 1870s, the English took the game outside, changed the rules slightly, and began to play on grass. Lawn tennis was born. Two players, standing on opposite sides of a court, strike the ball back and forth across a net hung in the middle. The player who hits the ball over the net the most times before his or her opponent misses it or makes an error earns a point. The first player to earn four points, with at least a two-point advantage, wins the game. And the first player to win six games wins the set. Most tennis competitions are best-two-out-of-three set matches, although some championships are best of five, particularly for men.

The game soon proved very popular with both sexes. Variations of lawn tennis evolved, such as doubles, in which two teams of two players play each other. But it remained a game played primarily by the wealthy.

Only private clubs could afford to build and maintain grass courts. Grass courts required a lot of upkeep to remain playable, which cost a lot of money. That's why tennis remained a game for the wealthy for so long.

And since most wealthy people in the countries where tennis was popular were white, so were most tennis players. For many years, in fact, tennis players *had* to be amateurs, which meant that only those who didn't have to work very much could afford the time to play, all but making certain the game would remain a pastime of the wealthy and privileged.

Then in the 1920s, some players began to play for money and turned professional. This opened up the sport to those who otherwise wouldn't be able to play. By the late 1960s, most big tournaments allowed professionals.

At the same time, many cities began to build and maintain public courts. Lawn tennis began to be played on other surfaces that were easier to maintain, like clay, and so-called hard courts, which are similar to pavement. These factors all combined to make the game accessible to everyone.

The first great African-American tennis player was a woman named Althea Gibson. In 1956, she became the first African American to win one of the four Grand Slam tournaments when she won the French Open. The other Grand Slam tournaments are the Australian Open, Wimbledon, and the U.S. Open. Gibson later won both the U.S. Open and Wimbledon. A decade later, the African American Arthur Ashe emerged from the public courts of St. Louis to become one of the best players in men's tennis, winning the U.S. Open in 1968, the Australian Open in 1970, and Wimbledon in 1975.

Despite the success of Ashe and Gibson, very few African Americans played tennis. Most people first learn a sport from friends and family. So few African Americans had played the game that there was little tennis tradition to build on.

Richard Williams began his own tennis tradition.

After learning the game himself, he taught all his daughters and his wife to play. But Brandi and the older girls didn't enjoy the game as much as Richard did. When Venus and Serena were born, Williams decided he would teach his two youngest daughters how to play the game when they were still young. He believed that if they started early enough, each might someday become a professional player. A year after he began taking Venus to the courts, he started teaching Serena as well.

After he taught the girls how to strike the ball, he began to teach them the rules of the game and basic tennis strategy. Soon the two girls began playing against each other.

The Williams sisters were tennis players.

Chapter Two:
1985–1991

Potential Prodigy

Soon Venus and Serena were in the park with their father every day, playing and practicing for hours. But Richard Williams knew he couldn't force the sport on his children. He made it clear to each that there were other things in life and that they were free to stop playing anytime they wished.

But they loved the game. Each looked forward to playing tennis every day.

Tennis was important to them, but it wasn't the only thing in their lives. When the girls started to attend school, their parents made certain that they learned that nothing was more important than education. In the Williamses' house, getting a B wasn't good enough. Richard and Brandi Williams expected their daughters to get A's. In fact, tennis practice depended upon how well they did in school. If they didn't earn an A, they weren't allowed to play tennis.

While both girls were good students and school proved to be no impediment to their tennis careers, other, more serious problems plagued their progress. Richard Williams and his daughters soon discovered that learning to play tennis in Compton could be dangerous.

Many young men and women in their neighborhood joined gangs. They sold drugs, battled one another, and ruled the streets through violence and intimidation. Various gangs divvied up the neighborhood and didn't allow others into their territory.

Compton's public parks became battlegrounds. Gangs often took over a park and wouldn't allow others to use the facilities.

On numerous occasions gang members told Richard that he and his girls weren't welcome. They often used the public spaces to sell drugs and indulge in other criminal activities. They didn't want anyone around to witness their crimes, not even a father and his daughters playing tennis.

But Richard Williams would not be dissuaded. He stood up to the gangs and for his right to use the parks. Over time, he and his daughters became accepted.

But the parks were still dangerous places to be. When gangs had disagreements with one another they generally resorted to violence to settle their differences. They fought one another in so-called drive-by attacks, using a car to ambush members of an opposing gang and shooting at them with automatic weapons. Such attacks often injured or killed innocent bystanders.

Richard Williams worried about his daughters. Drive-by attacks often took place at parks where the gangs congregated. Williams told his daughters to drop to the ground the instant they heard gunfire.

One day when Venus and Serena were nine and eight years old, they and their father were practicing at East Compton Park. In the middle of practice, some young men drove by in a car, stuck a gun out the window, and started shooting.

Venus, Serena, and Richard dropped to the ground as bullets flew all around them. Gang members hanging out in the park started to run and hide. Seconds later, the car sped away.

Richard Williams and the girls soon rose from the

court. They were shaken by the incident, but undeterred. A few minutes later, they resumed practice.

The Williams sisters were not just good tennis players; they were good all-around athletes. Richard Williams encouraged them to participate in other sports like gymnastics and track and field, believing that the skills they would learn playing other sports would eventually help their tennis game. Venus excelled at running and at age eight ran a mile in only five minutes and twenty-nine seconds, a remarkable time for a child.

Richard Williams taught his children well and soon realized that they were ready to start competing. When the girls were about seven or eight, he began to enter them in junior tennis tournaments, first in and around Los Angeles and then throughout southern California.

From the very beginning, Venus and Serena stood out. Their race, talent, and anonymity combined to make the two girls the subject of intense scrutiny.

Most other children in junior tennis had learned the game in private clubs, and many had already received professional instruction. Many of them knew one another from private clinics and tennis camps.

There were few African-American players, and fewer still who had simply been taught the game by a parent and then entered a tournament. People looked suspiciously at the Williams sisters, who were usually several years younger than the other players. Some acted as if they didn't belong.

At an age when most young tennis players are still struggling to get the ball over the net on a consistent basis, Venus and Serena were much more accomplished. Most matches between very young players are decided by what are known as "unforced errors," mistakes made by the player striking the ball, either sending it out of bounds or into the net. "Forced errors," are a product of more sophisticated play and come when the opponent makes a shot that is difficult to hit back, or return.

But Venus and Serena had played tennis every day for years and had spent far more time on the court than most of their opponents. Richard Williams had taught his daughters a variety of shots, each of which they had practiced thousands of times in drills. He had also played each girl himself hundreds of times so they could understand tennis strategy. The girls had played each other on countless occasions.

They were very competitive and knew what it took to win a match.

Moreover, it was clear that each girl was a fabulous athlete, well coordinated, and strong. Each could already strike the ball powerfully and accurately with either a forehand or a two-handed backhand shot. And each girl possessed a powerful serve for her age. Venus and Serena were already better than most young players were. Compared to playing against each other, they found junior tennis easy.

Competing in United States Tennis Association tournaments for the age-twelve-and-under division in southern California, both Venus and Serena found success right away. They began to win immediately.

But despite their success and the fact that both girls enjoyed competing, Richard and Brandi Williams were wary of placing too much emphasis on the tournaments. They thought most tennis parents took the tournaments far too seriously. Many acted like stage parents, living vicariously through their children. Some parents were pushy with their children and took winning and losing far too seriously. They yelled at their kids after a loss and argued with tournament officials.

At the same time, some parents treated the Williamses poorly, ignoring them and acting as if they didn't belong in the tournaments. Part of the reason was simple jealousy — the girls were winning. But the Williamses also believed that some of the people they were coming into contact with at the tournaments were prejudiced.

When Venus was nine and Serena was eight, the girls learned that playing the same sport could put them in an uncomfortable position. Richard Williams didn't want his daughters competing directly against each other and rarely entered them in the same tournament. But at one junior tournament at Indian Wells in California, Serena upset those plans.

Richard had entered Venus in the tournament. Unbeknownst to him, Serena decided she wanted to play, too. She got a copy of the tournament entry form, filled it out, and entered herself. When Richard discovered what she had done, he reluctantly allowed her to compete.

The two girls shredded the competition and ended up in the finals playing against each other. Although Richard and Brandi were nervous wrecks watching the girls play against each other in a tournament, the Williams sisters were unaffected. Venus won, but neither girl was shaken up by the experience — they didn't think it was a big deal. They'd played each other many times at the park.

Soon Venus, fifteen months older than Serena and a more accomplished player, began getting a lot of attention. She won almost every tournament she entered, and her father realized that her skills had progressed beyond his ability to teach her. When he could afford it, he began sending her to a man named Richard Cohen, a teaching pro who specialized in working with children.

On one occasion, Venus was getting a lesson at a private court where Cohen taught. John McEnroe and Pete Sampras, two of the biggest stars in men's professional tennis, happened to be at the club and couldn't believe what they were seeing. They had never seen a player so young play such accomplished tennis.

On another occasion, tennis legend Jack Kramer saw Venus play. He thought she had to be fourteen years old. He was stunned to discover Venus was only ten!

Tennis insiders began whispering that Venus Williams was a tennis prodigy. In recent years, a number of very young players had become successful professionals, particularly in women's tennis. Two young players, Tracy Austin and Andrea Jaeger, became regular winners on the women's tour at age fourteen. Rising star Jennifer Capriati had turned professional at age thirteen, leading the United States Tennis Association to make a rule prohibiting any player from turning professional before age fourteen. Still, everyone was on the lookout for the next big star. The buzz throughout the tennis world was that Venus Williams just might be that star.

Nothing she did on the tennis court made anyone think differently. In 1990, when Venus was only ten years old, she won seventeen straight tournaments and captured the southern California twelve-and-under championship. She was even mentioned in a story in the *New York Times* about tennis prodigies.

The publicity suddenly made Venus Williams very popular. She began receiving invitations to all sorts of celebrity tournaments and exhibitions. Everyone wanted to see her play.

At one tournament, she played with Zina Garrison,

a successful African-American professional player. After hitting the ball with Venus, Garrison was effusive in her praise. "For ten years old, Venus is exceptional. She would have beaten the ten-year-old Zina into the ground." A well-respected tennis coach who tutored a number of women professionals said simply, "She's headed for Grand Slam titles."

Already, sports agents were making inquiries to Richard and Brandi, trying to position themselves to represent Venus if she continued to progress and became a pro. Even though she was still too young to do so, manufacturers of tennis equipment were already eager to have Venus endorse their products. Such endorsements could be very lucrative. If she became as good as some people believed she would, she stood to earn millions of dollars. An agent, who negotiates contracts in exchange for a percentage of their value, could make a lot of money representing her.

The Williamses were flattered by the attention, but they were cautious. They didn't want to rush their daughter into anything. Players who turned professional at a very early age had a history of burning out and having disappointing careers.

Some observers, seeing the agents swirl around

Venus and her parents, were critical. "What's happening to our sport?" said one former star. "How's that kid going to enjoy what a ten-year-old should enjoy?" Others blamed Richard Williams himself, thinking he was simply trying to make a fortune off his daughter. Even today, Richard Williams is a controversial figure. No other parent in tennis has ever been so deeply involved in his daughter's career. But no other parent has ever raised two daughters who have been so successful, either.

The Williamses tried to keep Venus shielded from the surrounding circus, but the pressure was relentless. Richard Williams later claimed that some unscrupulous agents were offering them houses, cars, and money for the opportunity to represent his daughter. Things got so bad that Williams finally hired a couple of attorneys to hold the agents at bay and sort through legitimate opportunities.

Every decision the Williamses made concerning Venus was placed under scrutiny. People in organized tennis weren't accustomed to dealing with someone like Richard Williams. Some questioned his motives and his decisions concerning his daughter's career and upbringing.

The Williamses were confident that they knew best how to raise their children. Richard sought out some respected tennis figures for advice, like Arthur Ashe, who commented, "Mr. Williams has a lot of common sense, and it's obvious he is devoted to his children." Williams said his primary concern wasn't with tennis but with giving his daughters "class and self-respect and making them outstanding citizens. If I can teach those things, it's like giving them pure gold, even if they don't play tennis." He gave the girls books to read about young athletes who had failed to keep things in perspective and gotten into trouble, so they would know the hazards that they might face.

At the same time, the Williamses knew that it was time to make some decisions. Venus's notoriety was making it difficult to remain in Compton. People thought they were wealthy, and they worried that the girls would be at risk if they remained there. And although the family was comfortable, they lacked the financial resources to relocate and ensure that Venus and Serena would receive proper coaching. They weighed a number of offers and pondered their daughters' futures.

Both parents decided it was time to back off for a while. "Venus is still young," said her father. "We want her to be a little girl while she is a little girl."

They decided to cut back on the number of tournaments both girls would play in and protected the girls' privacy as best they could, keeping the name of their elementary school a secret from the press. They made sure both their daughters knew that they could stop playing tennis anytime they wanted and do anything they wanted in their lives. But both girls insisted that they still liked tennis best.

In 1991, when Venus turned eleven years old, the family made a decision. They accepted some endorsement deals for tennis clothing, which enabled the family to move from Compton to Florida so Venus and Serena could attend the International Tennis Academy, where Jennifer Capriati had once trained. "Her skills have already passed me," said her father about Venus. "I need someone to give her better practice and take her to the next level."

It was time for the Williams sisters to start getting serious.

Chapter Three:
1991–1994

Tennis School

After relocating to Florida, Venus and Serena got busy.

In many ways, both girls had outgrown junior tennis. The southern California junior tennis circuit is widely considered to be the best in the nation, yet each girl had dominated the competition. When the family moved to Florida, Venus, as an eleven-year-old, was ranked number one in the fourteen-and-under group and had won sixty matches in a row. Serena, competing as a ten-year-old in the twelve-and-under group, had a record of forty-seven wins and only three losses. Clearly, they were ready to move on.

Tennis insiders believed that, although they had become dominant junior players while being coached by their father, it would be impossible for them to continue progressing without professional coaching. Rick Macci became their new coach at the International Tennis Academy.

During most of the day, Venus and Serena lived like normal kids. They went to school, rode bikes, listened to music, and did all the normal things kids do. But each day after school they went to the academy.

Tennis academies are like big schools to learn how to play tennis. Parents pay thousands of dollars to have their children coached by the best teachers in the game. Some young athletes even leave their families and live at such schools.

The academy system, while effective, is also controversial. Young athletes spend hour upon hour honing their skills, and some people don't think that's healthy. Critics cite the fact that some young players get burned out by all the work and lose their love for the game and their desire to play. They also charge that less talented players are often cast aside, which can be a humiliating experience.

While some products of such "tennis factories" have found professional success, a number of them, such as Jaeger and Austin, seemed to lose interest in the sport. After achieving some early success, the careers of both young women were virtually over by age twenty. Some blamed the academy system.

The Williamses were determined not to let this happen to their girls. That's why the entire family moved to Florida. They thought it was important that they all stay together to give Venus and Serena the emotional support they would need.

Serena and Venus were already accustomed to long hours of practice with their father, and they adjusted rapidly to their new schedule. Each girl practiced with Coach Macci and the other instructors for hours nearly every day.

They were incredibly athletic for their ages, but playing junior tennis hadn't really challenged them to increase their skill level; they had been able to win without learning much about the nuances of the game. To be successful professionals, Venus and Serena had to increase their skill level and learn the inner game of tennis, the strategy involved in shot-making.

There is much more to playing professional tennis than the simple ability to hit the ball over the net. A player must learn to read the opponent and anticipate where she is going to set up and how she is going to return each shot. She has to learn to hit a wide variety of shots, such as forehands, backhands, and lobs. She has to learn when to charge the net and hit volleys, which is a shot struck before the ball has hit the ground, and when to stay back and hit ground strokes — shots after the ball has bounced — from back at the baseline. She has to learn how to set up the opponent and position her on the other side of the court to strike winners — unreturnable shots.

She also has to learn how and when to put spin on the ball, particularly on the serve, the shot that begins each game. In tennis, it is possible to hit the ball with the racket held at an angle, causing the ball to curve or slice like a baseball. Such hits make it more difficult for the opponent to gauge precisely where the ball is going to go. The ball can also be hit with either backspin, which means the ball spins backward, or topspin, which makes it spin toward the opponent. To hit a backspin shot, a player strikes down on the ball. A ball with backspin hits the court softly and bounces up. To give a shot topspin, a player swings over the ball. Topspin shots stay low, dip, and shoot across the court.

A player must learn all of these elements of tennis so well that they can be done automatically, almost without thinking. On the court the ball sometimes travels more than one hundred miles per hour. If a player hesitates before taking a shot, or doesn't know what to do, there is rarely enough time to recover. A tennis match can last for hours, and a player must also develop the stamina to play at top speed for a long time.

The Williams sisters worked on all these skills at the academy. They spent hours practicing different shots and then putting them together in matches against other players. Some people believe the Williams sisters were simply born with the ability to play tennis. But no one becomes a great athlete without practice. While both have natural athletic ability, each has spent thousands of hours practicing those skills. As Rick Macci later told a reporter, the girls worked "six hours a day, six days a week. There wasn't a day they wouldn't hit two hundred serves."

Richard Williams often observed his daughters at the academy. He wanted to know what they were working on, and he also wanted to learn more about tennis himself. Eventually, however, he got into some conflicts with his daughters' instructors.

The academy teachers were accustomed to parents who simply turned their children over to them and let them control every aspect of their game. Richard Williams wanted to remain involved in his daughters' coaching.

The instructors at the academy wanted Serena and Venus to continue to participate in junior tennis tournaments both in Florida and nationally. They thought that the girls needed to play tournament tennis to prepare them for the rigors of professional tennis. Richard Williams disagreed.

He believed that too much emphasis on winning was unhealthy, and he thought that being raised in Compton had already given his girls the mental toughness they needed to succeed. He also believed that playing in junior tournaments exposed the girls to racism. Williams was sensitive to the fact that his daughters were virtually the only African Americans in every tournament they played in, and he believed on occasion they were the victims of unkind words and insensitive behavior because of their race.

The decision to take the girls out of the junior circuit was controversial, both among the sisters' coaches and throughout the tennis world. Some observers charged that Richard Williams was sabotaging his daughters' careers. Tennis legend Chris Evert even said later, "I don't agree with the path the Williamses have taken with their career. I still advise kids to play the juniors."

Instructors at the academy also disagreed with the decision, and after a period of time Richard Williams pulled the girls out. They then began to train with another famous coach, Nick Bolletieri, at his academy. But their father soon pulled the girls out of there, too. Although they returned to training with Rick Macci, Richard Williams oversaw their development and resumed his role as the girls' primary coach.

Tennis insiders shook their heads disapprovingly when they learned that Richard Williams was coaching his daughters again. They didn't think he had the skills or knowledge to help them advance their game and thought that without the proper coaching they'd stop improving. Since neither girl was playing in tournaments anymore, no one really knew if they were continuing to progress. In a funny way, that made people even more interested in the girls. Their lives contained an element of mystery. No one knew quite how good they were or whether their parents were making the right decisions.

What many people didn't understand was that the Williamses were an incredibly close family. Brandi Williams and her daughters were members of the Jehovah's Witnesses, a Christian religion that requires a sizable commitment from its members. The family also wanted the girls to remember where they came from and not lose their connection to the African-American community as they immersed themselves in the primarily white world of tennis.

More than anything else, however, the Williamses wanted to make sure their daughters realized there was more to life than tennis. Their parents often pulled them away from practice to go on spontaneous family outings or to do some extra studying when their grades fell off. "I can remember fifty times when [Richard Williams] called off practice because Venus's grades were down," Rick Macci once told a reporter.

Since the two sisters weren't competing in tournaments anymore, the press and people throughout the tennis world wondered how the sisters were progressing. Apart from the occasional exhibition, few people saw them play. At this point, because she was older and more accomplished, Venus Williams had gotten most of the attention from the press. Even though Richard Williams had been telling people for years that "Serena is going to be better," most had dismissed that statement as the boasting of a proud father.

Although the two girls were both supremely talented, they were different. Venus was taller and physically stronger. Her game was based on power and strength. Serena, although just as tenacious a competitor, wasn't quite as strong and had to develop a more well-rounded game.

The girls also differed in temperament. Brandi Williams considers Venus more of a free spirit, saying, "She can take or leave tennis." Serena, on the other hand, is more focused. "I like going out and beating up on people [on the tennis court]," she once said. While Richard Williams has always believed that both girls would be successful, he predicted that Serena was "destined" to be a champion and would win a Grand Slam title before Venus.

Even though the sisters often found themselves competing on the tennis court, off the court they were best friends, telling interviewers they didn't need other friends because they had each other. Their older sisters remember only one fight between the two girls, when they were about five and six years old.

At about the same time that Richard Williams decided to pull the sisters from junior tournament competition, he also decided to pull them from school. For several years the girls were taught at home with the assistance of tutors. They later attended and graduated from private Driftwood Academy, where each girl maintained a grade point average above 3.0 out of a possible 4.0.

But the Williamses knew it would be impossible to keep their daughters shielded from the outside world forever. In 1994 the Women's Tennis Association (WTA) came under a great deal of criticism. The career of one-time tennis prodigy Jennifer Capriati crashed and burned. She had turned pro at age thirteen and enjoyed several years of spectacular success. Then the pressure got to her. She abandoned the game, and at age eighteen ended up in drug rehabilitation. Many observers blamed the USTA and WTA for allowing her to become a professional at such a young age, before she was mature enough to handle it.

The WTA, which controls women's professional tennis, responded by changing the rules. They announced that beginning in 1995 no one would be allowed to turn professional before age sixteen, and even then would only be allowed to play a limited number of tournaments until she turned eighteen. But anyone who turned professional before the end of 1994 would be able to compete in professional events under the old rules, with no restrictions on the number of events they could play.

Venus Williams was fourteen years old. The Williamses had to make a decision.

Chapter Four:
1994

The Professional

As the new WTA rule was being debated in the press, Richard Williams was asked several times what he thought about it. He responded by saying, "I don't approve of any kid turning professional at fourteen," suggesting that any parent who allowed his child to do so "ought to be shot." He was joking about that, of course, but he was apparently making it clear that he had no plans to allow Venus to become a professional at such a young age.

Therefore, it came as a surprise when in October of 1994 the Williamses announced that Venus would, in fact, become a professional and compete in her first tournament in over four years. The decision was controversial, and the press reminded Richard Williams of his earlier statement in regard to the issue.

The Williamses explained that the new ruling changed the situation entirely. They simply wanted to make sure that they kept their options open. Her mother explained that Venus was turning pro just "for the sake of turning pro" and that they had no plans for her to compete on a regular basis. Richard Williams was ambivalent about the decision, saying, "I'm counting on Venus to make a wrong decision right," by not succumbing to the pressures of pro tennis. Rick Macci added, "It was my advice to the father that she test the waters now so they're in a better position to pick and choose later." Serena, they all decided, was still too young to make a similar move. She would have to wait and compete at some point under the new rules.

And even though Venus was turning pro, the family had no plans to allow her to embark on a full-time professional schedule. "She may play this one event and then not play for four months. It's not like she's going on the circuit full-time. This is just a barometer," said her mother.

But ultimately, the decision to turn pro was Venus's. She was well aware of her potential importance to the sport, saying, "I think I can change the game," a comment about not only her race but her strength and athleticism.

"Maybe a year ago I wasn't sure about this," she added, "but I guess right now I'm ready. It's a learning experience." While training with Rick Macci, she had progressed so much that he often had her play against his male students. There were no female students, apart from Serena, who could keep up with her. She was trying to do things on the tennis court that only the best professional women were doing. As Macci described it, "She tried to hit like Monica Seles," a player known for her powerful baseline game, "and to come in like Martina Navratilova," a legendary veteran known for charging the net and playing aggressively. "It's not an easy game she's playing."

Venus wasn't a little girl anymore. She stood six feet tall, taller than most other women professionals. She had matured and was making the transition in her life from a child to a young woman. Although with her long arms and legs and braces she still looked a little gawky, she was passing through adolescence without losing her coordination. Everyone in tennis looked forward to her debut. No one had ever jumped to professional tennis with so little experience playing tournament tennis in the juniors.

The Williamses wisely chose to have Venus begin her career in her home state of California, in the Bank of the West Classic at the Oakland Coliseum. The tournament, scheduled to begin on November 1, was one of the last events of the year, and therefore one of Venus's last chances to play before the new rules went into effect.

All eyes were on Venus as the tournament approached. WTA officials suggested that she make her debut in an afternoon match, when there would be fewer people in attendance. They thought Venus would feel less pressure that way.

But Venus's father and the International Management Group, the agency that both sponsored the tournament and hoped to sign Venus as a client, successfully resisted the suggestion. They wanted Venus's debut to take place in the limelight. Venus herself really didn't care one way or the other. "I don't like having a big row made over me," she said, "but I'm expecting lots of people to come and take a peek at me there."

All eyes were on Venus when she took the court

and began practicing. The world of women's tennis had never seen anyone quite like her before.

She stood out for nearly every reason imaginable — her size, race, age, and even her hairstyle! Venus wore her hair in cornrows decorated with hundreds and hundreds of multicolored beads.

Her opponent in the first round of the tournament was veteran Shaun Stafford. At twenty-five, Stafford was nearly twice Venus's age. Most observers expected Stafford, ranked fifty-eighth in the world, to win easily.

A crowd of nearly 1,000 fans turned out for the match, a good crowd for a first-round match. But in addition to the fans, there were also hundreds of members of the media from all around the world. Everyone wanted to see if Venus Williams was for real.

They soon discovered she was. Venus played confidently and aggressively. Her serve was powerful and accurate, equal to any in women's tennis, and she displayed a full complement of shot-making ability, including delicate drop shots, lobs, and volleys. She proved equally proficient at both the baseline game and charging the net.

From the very beginning, Venus had Stafford on her heels. Each time Stafford tried to test Venus with a difficult shot, Venus rose to the challenge and found a way to return the ball. Over the course of the match, Stafford grew impatient and made a number of unforced errors. She was playing like the novice, while Venus displayed the composure of a veteran.

Venus won the first set, 6–3, and her body language made it clear she wasn't close to running out of steam. She had prepared for this moment. When the match paused during changeovers, breaks when the players take a brief breather before changing sides, Venus didn't even bother to sit down and rest. She remained standing, saying later, "I don't believe in sitting down. I don't sit down when I practice for four hours."

But in the second set, Stafford settled down and began making some shots. Venus fell behind, 3–4. Many people in the stands nodded knowingly at one another. They thought Venus had put up a good fight but was no match for an experienced veteran.

Venus responded like a champion. She drew on her reserves of energy and went on the attack, roaring back to take the next two games. All of a sudden, it was match point. All Venus needed to win was one more point.

She stood behind the baseline in service position and bounced the ball on the court several times, settling her nerves and getting into a good rhythm. On the opposite side of the court, Stafford shifted her weight nervously from one foot to the other, holding her racket in front of her with both hands, trying to anticipate Venus's serve.

When a player holds service, or the responsibility for starting play, she has two chances to hit the ball over the net and land it inbounds. On their first serve, players generally strike the ball as hard as they can, knowing that if they strike the net or send the ball out of bounds they still have another chance. But when that happens, they have to be much more conservative with their second attempt. The ability to get the first serve in is important, like a baseball pitcher throwing the first pitch for a strike.

The crowd quieted as Venus held the ball in her left hand, rocked slightly on her toes, then threw the ball several feet in the air. She swung her racket

41

back and then over the top with her right arm, striking the ball squarely and sending it toward her opponent like a rocket.

The ball streaked over the net. Stafford reacted quickly, but Venus's powerful serve was too quick and Stafford's reaction just a split second too slow. Her weak return skidded into the net.

Venus giggled and threw her arms into the air. She had won 6–3, 6–4!

As the crowd cheered, she pranced to the net to congratulate her weary opponent, giggling and grinning. She looked fresh enough to play another match.

Everyone was impressed by her performance, including her opponent. After the match, Stafford said, "She moves extremely well for her height. For her to come out and play like that is impressive. Obviously, she'll only get better."

Accomplished veteran Pam Shriver concurred. "Venus played a mature match," she said. "She closed it out like she's been playing ten years. . . . It's going to be fun to watch her progress."

Venus had precious little time to celebrate her

Despite the pressure, Venus (front) and Serena can't help laughing after they almost collide during a doubles match at the 1999 U.S. Open.

Serena and Richard Williams watch Venus play in the quarterfinals of
Wimbledon 2000.

One has to win, the other has to lose: Serena (right) congratulates
Venus on winning their semifinal match at Wimbledon 2000.

Serena and Richard cheer on Venus as she plays — and defeats — Lindsay Davenport to become the winner of Wimbledon 2000.

Double team: Venus and Serena hold their trophy after winning the women's doubles tournament at Wimbledon 2000.

Their popularity rising like a rocket, Serena and Venus even have dolls made in their likenesses.

Serena and Venus confer when rain delays their doubles match at the
2000 U.S. Open.

The Williams sisters strike again, this time defeating Russia's Elena Likhovtseva and Anastasia Myskina in the second round of doubles in the 2000 Olympics.

Donning formal dresses and high heels instead of sneakers and tennis dresses, the Williams sisters attend the Laureus Sports Awards ceremony, celebrating sporting excellence and achievement.

Joint effort yields yet another trophy, this time the women's double
championship at the Australian Open 2001.

The Careers of Venus and Serena Williams

Venus Williams

Birthdate: June 17, 1980
Birthplace: Lynwood, California
Height: 6'1"
Weight: 160 lbs.

WTA Tour singles titles: 17 (and one Olympic title)
WTA Tour doubles titles: 7 (and one Olympic title)
Grand Slam titles: 3 singles, 4 doubles, 2 mixed doubles

Career highlights — singles

Winner:

2001: Miami, Hamburg, Wimbledon, Acura Classic

2000: Wimbledon, U.S. Open, Olympics, Stanford, San Diego, New Haven

1999: Oklahoma City, Miami, Hamburg, Italian Open, New Haven, Zurich

1998: Oklahoma City, Miami, Grand Slam Cup

WTA Tour ranking (season-ending, singles)

2000: 3; 1999: 3; 1998: 5; 1997: 22; 1996: 204; 1995: 204

Highest singles ranking: 3 (August 30, 1999–November 26, 2000)

- In just her fourth tournament of 2000, she captured her first Grand Slam singles title at Wimbledon, becoming the second black woman to win title (Althea Gibson won in 1957 and 1958); defeated world no. 1 Martina Hingis in the quarterfinals, her sister Serena in the semifinals, and world no. 2, defending champion Lindsay Davenport, in the final.
- When she won 2000 Wimbledon, she and 1999 U.S. Open–champion sister Serena became the first sisters in tennis history to each win a Grand Slam singles title.
- Captured her second career Grand Slam singles title at the 2000 U.S. Open, which her sister Serena had won a year earlier. Defeated no. 2 Lindsay Davenport in the final to win her fifth consecutive tournament and extend her match winning streak to 26.
- In 2000 won the Olympic gold medal in singles and doubles, joining Helen Wills in 1924 as the only women to win both in medal competition.
- From July 1 through October 15, 2000, she or her sister Serena won eight of the nine tournaments they entered.
- Captured first pro singles title in 1998 in Oklahoma City, defeating top seed and world no. 2 Lindsay Davenport in the semifinals and fourth seed Joannette Kruger in the final.
- Recorded the fastest serve in WTA Tour history at 1998 Zurich Open with a 127 mph ace on match point against Mary Pierce.
- By age 12, had accumulated a 63–0 record in USTA sectional play in Southern California.

Serena Williams

Birthdate: September 26, 1981
Birthplace: Saginaw, Michigan
Height: 5'10"
Weight: 145 lbs.

Career highlights — singles
Winner: 2001: Indian Wells; 2000: Hannover, Los Angeles, Tokyo [Princess Cup]; 1999: U.S. Open, Paris Indoors, Indian Wells, Los Angeles, Grand Slam Cup

Career highlights — doubles
Winner (8): 2001: Australian Open (with Venus Williams); 2000: Wimbledon (with Venus Williams), Olympics (with Venus Williams); 1999: French Open (with Venus Williams), U.S. Open (with Venus Williams), Hannover (with Venus Williams); 1998: Oklahoma City (with Venus Williams), Zurich (with Venus Williams)

WTA Tour ranking (season-ending, singles)
2000: 6; 1999: 4; 1998: 20; 1997: 99

Highest singles ranking: 4 (September 13, 1999–March 19, 2000)

• When her sister Venus won 2000 Wimbledon it marked the first time in tennis history that two sisters had each won a Grand Slam singles title.
• Won the gold medal in doubles at the 2000 Olympics with her sister Venus, becoming the first sisters to win the Olympic doubles event.
•From July 1 through October 15, 2000, she or her sister Venus won eight of the nine tournaments they entered.
• Won five WTA Tour singles titles in 1999, including the U.S. Open.
• In 1999, did not have a losing record against any player ranked in the top 5.
• Upset no. 1 Martina Hingis, no. 2 Lindsay Davenport, and no. 4 Monica Seles to win first career Grand Slam singles title at the 1999 U.S. Open, becoming the lowest seed to win the women's title and the second black woman ever to win a Grand Slam singles title (Althea Gibson won five).
• Along with sister Venus, became the first sisters to meet in a WTA Tour final, in 1999 at Miami; lost to Venus in three sets.

victory. The win earned her the right to play the next day against Aranxta Sanchez Vicario, who was ranked number two in the world and seeded number one in the tournament, meaning that officials gave her the best chance of winning. She was one of the best women's tennis players in the world. Absolutely no one believed Venus would beat Vicario or even give her much of a test.

No one told that to Venus. From the very beginning, she played to win.

In the first set, Venus came out and aggressively attacked, making use of her advantage in speed and power to keep Vicario from getting comfortable. Time and time again, Venus's powerful serves and strong returns rocketed past her more experienced opponent. Venus won the first set easily, 6–2.

Her momentum carried forth into the second set, and she jumped out to a quick 3–1 lead. If Venus could win another three games, she'd win the match and reach the quarterfinals in her very first pro tournament!

But Vicario didn't panic. Venus had expended a great deal of energy, and Vicario sensed that she was beginning to get tired. Vicario settled into the match and used her experience and superior shot-making ability to come back to win, 6–3. The match would be decided in the third set.

Venus quickly fell behind, but she didn't quit. Even though Vicario ended up winning every game, shutting out Venus, 6–0, to win the match, Venus never gave up. On several occasions she fought Vicario to deuce, meaning each had won three points, tying the score at 40–40. And in the third game, despite being down 15–40, Venus took the game to two break points before losing.

After she congratulated Vicario on her victory, Venus still had enough poise to thank the crowd for their support. "Folks," she said, "I've had a lot of fun. I just wanted to say to Aranxta, 'You played great.'" Vicario gave Venus a hug and added, "You, too." Then she let out a great big sigh of relief. She knew that Venus had nearly pushed her to the limit.

It had been an auspicious start for Venus Williams. She had played well and taken the tournament in stride, proving that she belonged and vindicating her father's training methods and the decision to turn pro. As Venus said in a press conference after the match, "I wasn't nervous at all tonight. I had nothing to lose, nothing to win. I was just having fun."

In the next few years, Venus would have a lot more fun. And so would Serena.

Chapter Five:
1995–1997

Tourney Time

Women's tennis needed the Williams sisters. After years of growing popularity, the sport had started to slip.

For many years, women's tennis was almost a fringe sport, one that few people paid much attention to. While men's champions became familiar names to most sports fans, women tennis players were nearly anonymous.

In earlier decades, female tennis players had to compete in long-sleeved shirts and long skirts, which hampered their play. After World War II, new styles of sportswear became acceptable. Shorter tennis skirts helped improve play, but women's tennis remained an obscure sport throughout the 1960s.

But in the 1970s women's tennis enjoyed a surge

in popularity that started with champion Billie Jean King. She played a different game from many of her forebears. King was aggressive on the court, adopting an exciting, attacking style of play that tennis fans enjoyed watching. She realized that as a champion she had the responsibility to help popularize her sport, and she worked tirelessly to do so, giving clinics and making other public appearances to raise the profile of the game.

In 1973, a former men's champion, Bobby Riggs, created quite a stir. He didn't think much of women's tennis. Riggs, nearly sixty years old, challenged King to play.

The challenge captured the imagination of the media, and the two met in what was termed "The Battle of the Sexes," a televised exhibition that men and women from all over the world watched as if it were the Super Bowl. King stepped up to the challenge and beat Riggs easily. Spectators began to appreciate women's tennis and to take the sport more seriously.

The next great figure in women's tennis was Chris Evert. In a career that spanned from 1972 through 1989, Evert won 157 tournaments, including eighteen

Grand Slam titles. Fans loved her steady, tenacious game and good looks. Evert built on what King had begun and drew many new fans to the sport. In the 1970s, thousands of tennis courts were built all over the country as the sport experienced a tremendous boom.

In the 1980s, Evert and Martina Navratilova, a Czechoslovakian native who defected to the United States, created one of the greatest rivalries of all of sports. Each brought out the best in the other. Navratilova's power game contrasted nicely with Evert's baseline game, and the two fought many memorable battles on the court. Eventually, Navratilova got the better of Evert. Many consider her the greatest women's tennis player ever.

In the late 1980s and early 1990s, it appeared as if a new generation of women's tennis stars were ready to take over and build on the accomplishments of King, Evert, and Navratilova. But after Jaeger, Austin, and Capriati burned out, and emerging champion Monica Seles was injured when she was attacked by a mentally ill fan, there was suddenly a void in women's tennis. While there were still many talented players, such as Steffi Graf, Sanchez Vicario, and others, none had that special extra spark that drew new fans to the sport, particularly in the United States. The sport needed a new generation of players to take over.

Many believed that Venus Williams would be the next big star in women's tennis. Her background demonstrated that anyone could make it in tennis and that you didn't have to be wealthy to play. African Americans who had paid little attention to the sport before began to track her progress. People who weren't tennis fans could relate to her.

A star like Venus could broaden the game's appeal and get people interested in tennis again. To accomplish that, she would have to fulfill her enormous potential and start winning. In the wake of her spectacular debut, everyone thought the Williamses would be unable to resist the lucrative lure of professional tennis. There were millions of dollars to be made in endorsements, as well.

But her family surprised many when they continued their cautious and conservative approach to her career. After making her debut, Venus returned to Florida and resumed her usual routine — going to school and playing tennis with her sister and at Rick

Macci's academy. In all of 1995, she played in only three minor tournaments. And while she did accept some endorsement opportunities, she turned down far more than she accepted.

In September of 1995, Serena turned fourteen years old. Although she was too young to play professionally in the WTA, the Williamses decided that she, too, would turn pro by playing in an unsanctioned professional tournament. As they had with Venus, they wanted to keep Serena's options open. And since she wasn't competing in junior tournaments anyway, there was no reason to retain her amateur status.

She made her debut at a small tournament in Quebec, Canada. She wasn't as well known as Venus, and her appearance didn't cause a big stir. She stood several inches shorter than her sister and wasn't quite as rangy. She had her own style of play, too. She didn't have the power game that Venus had. Hers was more of a baseline, serve-and-volley style of tennis.

Facing eighteen-year-old Anne Miller, Serena played well but was badly beaten, losing in straight sets, 6–1, 6–1. Then, like Venus the year before, Serena went back to Florida and resumed her usual routine.

But even though the sisters weren't playing much competitive tennis, they kept busy. They were now teenagers, and they liked to do the same things most girls their age do.

Both girls loved music and kept up with all the popular bands, buying CDs, listening to the radio, and watching videos. They spent a lot of free time with their pet dogs, and both looked forward to learning how to drive when they turned sixteen.

Each sister was a great student at school. They were curious about everything. Since tennis is an international sport, Venus and Serena both studied Italian and French. They'd later surprise some members of the foreign press by responding to questions in both languages.

Life continued more or less the same through 1996. But when Venus turned sixteen in 1997, she was able to play more regularly.

In July she made her first appearance at Wimbledon, an English tournament based at the All-England Lawn Tennis Club. Wimbledon, one of the few competitions still played on grass, is the most famous tennis tournament in the world. Venus had long dreamed about playing there. Many tennis observers expected her to do well.

Playing against Magdalena Grzybowska, Venus rolled to a 6–4 win in the first set and staked out a 2–0 lead in the second. Then she suddenly fell apart. Grzybowska's backhand mystified Venus, who lost, 6–4, 2–6, 4–6. As one sportswriter noted, "Williams stood revealed as a huge talent with little idea how to adjust to an opponent." But Venus was philosophical, saying, "It's my first Wimbledon. There will be many more."

Despite the loss, Venus continued to improve. At the U.S. Open in September, she announced to the world that she was just about ready to start winning.

Despite not being seeded at the tournament, she battled her way into the finals against Martina Hingis. Although Hingis hammered her in the finals, 6–0, 6–4, everyone, including Hingis, was impressed by Venus's play. "She got better and better," said Hingis. "For the first time she showed she can play great."

Although Venus didn't win a tournament that year, she advanced to the quarterfinals in two competitions, moving up in the WTA rankings from 211 to 64, a spectacular improvement that definitely marked her as a rising star.

At the same time, Serena began to make people take notice, too. At Chicago, in only her fifth professional tournament, she defeated two of the top-ten players in the world, Mary Pierce and Monica Seles, becoming the lowest-ranked player ever to defeat two top-ten players in the same tournament.

But as the sisters began playing better tennis, they found themselves under increased scrutiny. Players who were far more accomplished were jealous of the attention they received. In addition, the confident Williams sisters didn't act with the deference that many people in tennis expected. This attitude irritated some observers.

Others were put off by the Williamses' insistence on reminding everyone that they were black women playing what most people still perceived as a white person's game. Richard Williams, whose outspokenness on a variety of issues hadn't made him very popular with the tennis establishment to begin with, seemed to go out of his way to bring up the issue. But while Venus and Serena still had a lot to learn about professional tennis and handling the press, pro tennis and the press also had a lot to learn about them. As Venus said at a press conference at the U.S. Open, "I'm tall, I'm black. Everything's different about me. Just face the facts."

And the fact was that the Williams sisters were on the rise. Women's tennis would never be the same again.

Chapter Six:

Breaking Through

It didn't take Venus and Serena very long to get everyone's attention in 1998. Serena joined her sister on the WTA tour full-time, and in January both chose to compete in the Australian Open. To prepare for the tournament, they played in a warm-up event, the Adidas International in Sydney.

In the second round of the tournament, Venus had to play number-one ranked Martina Hingis. As Hingis had noted at the U.S. Open, Venus was getting better and better. She soon provided evidence that this was still true.

After losing the first set, 3–6, Venus remained poised and stuck to her game. She bounced back to knock off Hingis, 6–4, in the second set and led in the third. On the precipice of victory, however, she had to ask for a break.

In her excitement, Venus had forgotten to drink enough water. With victory in sight, her body was suddenly wracked by cramps. As she was treated at courtside, tears rolled down her face.

Most observers thought she was crying in pain, but she wasn't. She was crying because she thought she was going to have to quit.

Fortunately, her cramps subsided, and she was able to resume the match. She picked up right where she left off and rolled to a tough 7–5 win to defeat Hingis.

The tennis world was shocked. Never before had a player ranked number one been defeated in her first match of the season.

They received another shock a short time later. Serena's first match was against Lindsay Davenport, the tournament's second seed and one of the best players in the world. Serena easily defeated her.

Tennis fans looked forward to the possibility of an all-sisters final, but it was not to be — yet. Although Venus made it to the finals, Serena lost in the semifinals. Aranxta Sanchez Vicario won the tournament.

Although both sisters were happy to have played well, there was little time to celebrate. The Australian Open began a few days later.

In tournament play, players are matched up, or seeded, in various groups called brackets, according to their rank in the tennis world. The two highest-ranked players are in separate brackets. They play each other only if they make it to the finals. Non-seeded players are distributed throughout the tournament according to a draw.

In the Australian Open, Venus and Serena discovered that if they each won their first-round match, they'd have to play each other in the second round! Sure enough, each won her opening match.

Although they had practiced against each other countless times and played each other in juniors, playing each other in a professional tournament was another matter entirely. Each girl wanted to win every time she stepped on the court, but each wanted her sister to win as well. The situation made both a little uncomfortable.

There was a huge crowd at center court for the second-round matchup. But the crowd was uncharacteristically quiet, as if sensing that neither player was particularly eager to play.

Venus and Serena were both tense, and it showed in their play. Each made a number of unforced errors in the first set. For a while, it seemed as if neither sister really wanted to win.

With the set tied at 6–6, Venus finally got an edge. After a long rally, Serena sent a forehand wide. Venus took advantage and won a tiebreaker, 7–4, to take the set, 7–6.

The defeat seemed to make Serena lose confidence. She kept double-faulting on her serve. Venus won the second set, 6–1, to take the match.

But Venus didn't jump for joy at her victory. She met her sister at the net and gave her a hug, and then the two sisters held hands and bowed together to the crowd. As they walked off the court, still holding hands, Venus said softly to Serena, "I'm sorry I had to take you out. I didn't want to, but I had to."

Serena took the loss in stride. "If I had to lose in the second round, there's no one better to lose to than Venus." When a reporter asked Venus if the match was fun, she sighed and said, "Was it fun? I think it would have been great fun if it were the final. It was a match, a tough match. Serena's a great player. She hasn't played that much, and she's taken people out left and right. . . . Serena hates to lose, and her reputation is that she doesn't lose to anyone twice, so I'm going to be practicing secretly if I want to win the next one."

Venus went on to the quarterfinals before losing, but she wasn't quite finished with the Australian Open. There was still the doubles competition.

Doubles is a variation of tennis in which two teams of two players play against each other. In big tournaments, there are doubles competitions for men and women, and mixed doubles, with a man and woman on each team.

Venus paired up with Justin Gimelstob in mixed doubles, and the two were the surprise of the field, winning the championship with ease. Although the win wasn't as important as the singles title, it was still a big victory and represented Venus's first win in a Grand Slam event.

The girls' performance in Australia got the attention of the tennis world. From now on, it was clear that they were a threat to win every time they stepped on the court. The only question that remained was exactly when that would happen.

Two months later, Venus provided the answer. Playing in the IGA Tennis Classic in Oklahoma City, she dumped Lindsay Davenport in the semi-finals to reach the finals. She was one victory away from her first singles win in a professional tournament.

She obliterated Joannette Kruger, 6–3, 6–2 to capture the title and win $27,000. "This is one I'll always remember," she said afterward. "This shows me what it's like to win, what it takes to win." That was a lesson she wouldn't soon forget. The win vaulted her all the way up to a number twelve ranking.

Throughout the remainder of the 1998 season, both Venus and Serena made tremendous strides. Venus, in particular, just kept getting stronger as her body filled out. When she started on the women's tour, her serve was just a little better than average. As she matured and grew stronger, however, she learned how to transfer more strength to the ball. In one tournament in 1998, her serve was timed at 127 miles per hour.

That was the fastest serve in women's tennis. In fact, that was more powerful than the serve of many male players.

Such a powerful service gave Venus a tremendous advantage. When a player is serving and the opponent is unable to successfully return a serve, it is referred to as an "ace" and is worth a point. Venus's opponents were not accustomed to returning such serves, and Venus could often use her serve to score. And even when her opponents were able to return her serve, they often did so defensively and either made an error or returned it weakly, allowing Venus to attack.

Some members of the women's tour complained that playing Venus was like playing a man. But Venus made no excuses for her skill. Her powerful serve was a product of hard work and hours spent practicing on the court and in the gym. As men's champion Andre Agassi commented, "She's the best athlete the woman's game has seen. Now it's a matter of how she puts it all together."

Venus had improved dramatically. She rarely lost to players ranked below her and in most tournaments reached the quarterfinals easily. She picked up another win in the Lipton Championships, beating teen sensation Anna Kournikova, and made it to the semifinals of the U.S. Open before losing to Lindsay Davenport.

Serena nearly kept pace with her sister. In almost every tournament she played, she knocked off higher ranked players. Although she failed to capture a title, before most tournaments she had the opposition poring over the brackets to see if there was any chance they might have to play her.

That included Venus. In the Italian Open, the sisters met for a second time. Serena, playing on a clay court for the first time, had beaten three players ranked above her in order to face her sister. But Venus proved to be the stronger player, beating her sister again.

The Williams sisters' improvement sparked a popular revival of women's tennis. They were part of a new generation of female players who captured the imagination of fans. Competition had never been tougher, as a half dozen or more players in each tournament had a good chance to win every time they played. Number-one ranked Martina Hingis was the most accomplished player in the game, followed by other young stars like Davenport, Mary Pierce, and Anna Kournikova and veterans Steffi Graf and Monica Seles. Women's tennis had rarely been so competitive. There was more interest in the sport than there had been in years.

But the sisters' rise to the top was not without its rough spots. In the French Open, Serena made it into the fourth round, and then had to face Aranxta Sanchez Vicario, one of the best players in the world on clay.

After her experience in the Italian Open, Serena was more comfortable playing on the surface. Early on she appeared to have the match under control, displaying an absolutely breathtaking variety of shot-making skills. When she needed to slam a backhand winner, she did so with ease, but when she needed to make a more delicate shot, like a lob or a drop, she quickly adjusted. Sanchez Vicario was off balance.

Late in the match, Serena hit a return that Sanchez Vicario argued had bounced twice before she hit it, an infraction of the rules. As Sanchez Vicario pled her case to the referee, Serena approached the net, and the two got into an argument. The referee refused to change the call and on the next point, Serena won the first set, 6–4. Sanchez Vicario slammed her racket to the ground in anger.

In the second set, however, Serena ran out of steam. Sanchez Vicario came back to win the second set.

In the third set, Serena was losing when she inadvertently struck a shot that nearly hit her opponent. Sanchez Vicario took offense. After winning the match, she let everyone know how she felt about Serena.

She thought Serena had behaved too aggressively. "She cannot have that attitude," she complained. "I'm glad I beat her. I taught her a lesson."

But Serena was far more diplomatic. She didn't apologize for playing hard. She and Venus were accustomed to having opponents question their style of play and competitiveness. "Everything is a learning experience for me," she said.

And the sisters *were* learning. When they started to play professionally, they had been strangers to almost everyone. Many of the other players had known one another for years after playing together in the juniors. They were all friends.

For a while, Venus and Serena stuck to each other like the best friends they were. It wasn't easy to build relationships with other players, most of whom were several years older. But as each sister grew older and played more, they depended a little less on each other and grew more comfortable around other people.

By the end of the year, they had established themselves in the WTA. Venus ended the year ranked number six, and Serena, after only one full season of tournament play, was ranked number twenty.

There was still room for improvement.

Chapter Seven:
1999

We Are Family

Both girls were becoming more independent. In 1999, they decided to play separate schedules. Apart from the Grand Slam events and a few others, they'd rarely play in the same tournament. It was hard to compete against each other, and doubly hard on their parents. No matter which daughter won, one still had to lose. As Serena later explained, "We're just trying to stay away and just trying to get more experience first and both just trying to get a better ranking right now. It was just a mutual decision. Something the whole family talked about and decided it would be best for us and the sport."

Serena and Venus thrived on their own. In late February and early March, they made history.

Serena chose to play the Gaz de France Open in

Paris. At the same time, Venus was competing in the IGA Classic in Oklahoma City.

Each kept up with the other's progress over the Internet. After each match, they excitedly e-mailed each other about their performances. Each raced through the early rounds and made it to the finals.

On March 1, Serena faced Amelie Mauresmo in the Gaz de France Open final. She was still looking for her first tournament victory. After winning the first set, 6–2, she lost the second, 3–6. It all came down to the final set.

Serena jumped ahead 4–1, but Mauresmo fought back to make it close. The match went to a tiebreaker before Serena fired an ace at 5–3 to take control. She went on to win, 7–6 (7–4).

"I've always dreamed of winning Grand Slams, and this is a start," said Serena later. "It's good to win a smaller tournament because when I get to the big events I will have the experience." It was also good to win the $80,000 that came with the victory. She immediately sent her sister an e-mail to give her the good news.

Half a world away in Oklahoma, Venus learned of

her sister's win before she took the court herself in search of her own victory. "I found out she won before I came out to play my match," she said. "I really felt it was my duty to come out here and win."

She got right to work versus Amanda Coetzer. In a stunning performance, she dispatched her opponent in only fifty-eight minutes, winning 6–4, 6–0.

Richard Williams, who accompanied Venus to Oklahoma while Brandi went with Serena to France, was ecstatic. "It makes me think about where we came from, out of the ghetto. To have them both win brought tears to my eyes."

Now that Serena had broken through with a win, she was eager for more. It didn't take her very long.

One week later at Indian Wells, Venus watched as Serena dominated the field, winning every match she played to collect her second win and $200,000. Serena acknowledged that it helped her knowing she wouldn't have to face her sister. "I don't have to worry about meeting her," she said. "It definitely changed my feelings [toward the tournament]. I know I can go all the way."

But it was impossible for the sisters to avoid each other entirely. Each decided to play in the lucrative

Lipton Championships at the end of March. As the two hottest players in the WTA, each knew there was a good chance they might meet.

When the draw came out, the girls saw that the only way they would face each other would be if they met in the finals.

This time, both sisters looked forward to that possibility. They had grown and matured, and each was at the top of her game. "The way we're playing, it's inevitable," said Venus.

But it wouldn't be easy. Although both proceeded to the semi-finals without really being tested, each met a tough competitor there. Venus faced Steffi Graf and Serena went up against Monica Seles.

Although the girls were looking ahead to the finals, they were able to maintain their focus. Venus dominated Graf, beating her in straight sets, 6–2, 6–4. Serena dumped Seles, 6–2, 6–3. The sisters would meet in the finals!

Their accomplishment didn't go unnoticed. Sisters hadn't faced each other in the finals of a major tournament since Maud and Lilian Watson played each other at Wimbledon in 1884. All of a sudden, everyone seemed to recognize that the Williams

sisters were as good as their father had been pre-
dicting they would be. "With their power and
ground strokes, they have a tough combination,"
said Seles. "I think the other players are seeing that."

"Everything's working for them," added Graf.
"They go for their shots, they're taking risks, and
they don't really have a weakness."

Both seemed to look forward to the matchup.
"I've always been in the background," said Serena.
"It's time for me to move forward."

Venus wasn't so sure about that. "I don't like
putting my name and losing in the same sentence,"
she said. "Winning and Venus sounds great."

When Venus and Serena took the court for the final, the atmosphere was electric. The old hit song
"We Are Family" by Sister Sledge blared over the
loudspeakers. The crowd was unlike any other ever
seen at a WTA final. People of all ages and colors
packed the stands to witness history. The sisters had
captured the imagination of the tennis world. Little
girls stood in long lines to get their hair beaded
and braided. Richard Williams was totally unable
to contain his pride as he paraded through the

stands with a sign that said WELCOME TO THE WIL-LIAMS SHOW.

That's exactly what it was. The match was one of the most anticipated in the world of tennis, and millions watched on television.

But once again, the sisters found that playing each other caused some special problems. As one writer noted, the result was a "great story, but lousy tennis." Nerves seemed to get the better of them.

Serena had been playing great tennis, winning sixteen matches in a row, and was favored by many to win. But in the opening set, she had a hard time getting her head in the game. Venus didn't play very well either, but still managed to win, 6–1.

Both sisters settled down in the second set, however. Serena fought hard and won, 6–4. The match would be decided in the final set.

Finally, the sisters gave spectators a glimpse of the kind of tennis they had tuned in to see.

Down 2–4 in the final set, Serena suddenly rallied. In the seventh game of the set, she demonstrated just how badly she wanted to win.

In the midst of one long rally, Serena hit a forehand

out of bounds. She reacted by throwing her racket toward her courtside chair. It bounced wildly and struck a television cameraman, earning her a warning.

A few minutes later, in another long rally, Venus charged the net. Serena came back with a hard forehand smash.

Thwack! The ball struck Venus on the wrist. Both sisters were playing as hard as they could.

Serena fought back to tie the set at 4 all, but the effort seemed to exhaust her. She lost eight of the next nine points to lose the set 4–6, and the match. Venus was the Lipton champion.

She didn't celebrate her win, though. She simply walked expressionless to the net, slapped hands softly with her sister, then put her arms around her. The two walked off the court together.

Venus's victory was bittersweet. She knew that her sister felt bad about losing to her again. "Family comes first, no matter how many times we play each other," she said. "Nothing will come between me and my sister. In the end we go home, we live life. You have to remind yourself it's a game, and there's only one winner."

But Serena wasn't ready to give up. "I'm definitely looking forward to another final with Venus," she said. "Now that my game is taken to a different level, it's going to happen more. It's what we've always dreamed of." Indeed, both sisters were now ranked in the top ten. They were a threat to win every tournament they played.

The Williams show was ready to go on the road.

Chapter Eight:
1999

Slamming Sister

Both Serena and Venus resumed their usual schedules. They played in different tournaments, and each continued to play well. With the 1999 French Open, Wimbledon, and U.S. Open all still to be played, most observers expected one of the sisters, if not both, to win her first Grand Slam event. Perhaps they'd even face each other in one of the finals.

In May, Venus played in the Italian Open. Although the Open isn't considered a Grand Slam event, the clay court championship usually draws a strong field. The French Open, another clay court tournament, is held only a few weeks later, and many players use the Italian tournament to adjust to the surface.

Playing on clay was a challenge to Venus. Her powerful game wasn't suited to the slower surface.

Strategy and finesse were more important on clay than strength.

Still, just the week before against weaker competition in Hamburg, Germany, Venus had surprised everyone by capturing her first clay court title. Observers still weren't sure if the victory was a fluke or whether her overall game had evolved. Venus looked forward to demonstrating that her win hadn't been an accident.

Adjusting her style to suit the clay surface. Venus played strong and steady tennis in the early rounds and found herself in the finals opposite Mary Pierce, a player known for her prowess on clay. Pierce would provide a good challenge.

Venus showed amazing focus during the match. At various times a swarm of bees moved through the stands, an airplane buzzed the court, and the loudspeaker system was plagued by feedback. Nevertheless, Venus retained her composure and stayed patient. She used a strong serve to put Pierce on the defensive and then played a baseline game, waiting for Pierce to tire and make some unforced errors.

The plan worked to perfection and Venus won, 6–4, 6–2. She entered the French Open a big favorite, and the sisters again faced the possibility that they might have to play each other.

It didn't happen. Although they won the women's doubles championship together, in singles competition Serena lost in the third round and Venus was booted in the fourth. A Grand Slam title would have to wait. The sisters set their sights on the lush grass surface of Wimbledon.

The draw was announced. If Serena and Venus each made it through the first three rounds, they would face each other in round four. But when the sisters arrived in England, nothing went as planned.

Just before the beginning of the tournament, Serena contracted the flu and was forced to withdraw. There would be no Williams-Williams showdown on center court.

Serena's withdrawal appeared to open the door for Venus. Her path to the finals suddenly seemed a lot easier.

Then Venus, too, came down with a touch of the flu. Although she was still able to play, at the beginning of the tournament she felt weak and sluggish.

Nevertheless, she fought through the illness and made it to the quarterfinals against Steffi Graf. Graf had won the French Open and was playing well at Wimbledon. Many people thought that whoever won the quarterfinal match would probably win the tournament.

Venus and Graf were both at the top of their game. The result was a memorable and grueling match.

The weather was poor, and the match was halted several times by rain. The three-set classic took an amazing seven hours to complete. But the result was disappointing to Venus. She lost, 2–6, 6–4, 3–6.

The sisters began to look ahead to the U.S. Open, played in early September. The tournament would be the last time the two would play in the same tournament in 1999 and the last chance either would have to win a Grand Slam title that year.

The setting was perfect for a victory by one of the Williams sisters. A victory on their home soil would be appropriate. The tennis facility at Flushing Meadow, New York, had recently been rebuilt and renamed after Arthur Ashe, the trailblazing African-American men's champion who had passed away several years before. There was no better place in the world for a Williams to win.

When the draw for the Open was announced, Venus was seeded number three and Serena number seven. They were in different brackets, and that set up the possibility of an all-Williams final. "I hope it works out that way," said Venus. "It would be great."

Both sisters were playing well. Each made it to the semifinals with ease. The champion of the tournament would come from among the remaining four players — Serena, Venus, Lindsay Davenport, and Martina Hingis.

In the minds of many, those four women were the best four tennis players in the world. And each exhibited a slightly different style of play. Venus was all power and speed. Davenport was about the only other player on the WTA tour, apart from Serena, who could match her power, but she lacked Venus's quickness. Serena had the skills and shot-making ability to play both a power game and a baseline game, while the savvy Hingis was best known for her consistency and finesse. No matter who ended up in the final, a great tennis match seemed certain.

Serena faced Davenport in the first semifinal. In

order to win, she knew she'd have to keep her opponent on the move and wear her out. If she allowed Davenport to set up, her powerful returns could give Serena trouble.

Serena worked her game plan to perfection in the first set and won, 6–4. She was one set away from reaching the finals.

But in the second set she fell behind, then fell apart. The shots Serena had made with ease in the first set suddenly went awry. Davenport stormed back to defeat her, 6–1. With only one set remaining, Serena had to scramble to come up with a solution.

She found her answer in her serve. She started the match by serving three rockets for aces, stopping Davenport in her tracks. Now she had a chance.

The two players fought it out for the remainder of the set, but in the end Serena came out on top, winning, 6–4, to take the match and earn a place in the finals. "I just stayed determined and focused," she said later.

As the two left the court, Venus and Hingis took

over and began to practice. Serena showered, then rushed back to watch from the stands and cheer her sister on.

Martina Hingis plays a much more classic style of tennis than the Williams sisters. While Venus's serve is regularly timed at more than 120 miles per hour, and Serena's as much as 115 miles per hour, the diminutive Hingis can barely hit ninety miles per hour.

But she doesn't have to. Quick on her feet and blessed with a full repertoire of shots, the ever-confident Swiss player is particularly accomplished at returning serves and then settling in, taking her opponent on long rallies that she often ends by making precision shots just out of reach and just in bounds. She appears to be able to probe her opponent and discover precisely which part of her game isn't quite working on a given day, and then take advantage. Already, many of her matches against the Williams sisters had been classics, as the dramatic contrast in styles usually made for great tennis.

The eventual winner of a tennis tournament is determined by much more than the result of a single match. To reach the finals, a player sometimes has to play as many as seven or eight separate matches. The final result is often dependent upon how hard a player had to work earlier in the tournament. Players hope to reach the later stages of a tournament still feeling fresh.

In the first set against Venus, Hingis was at her best. Venus played well but was unable to make any headway. Hingis ran Venus all over the court and eventually came away with a 6–1 win. Although Venus lost six games, those games were actually much closer than the final score indicated.

But Venus didn't give in. Hingis had to work hard to win the first set, and Venus made her continue to work. Venus seemed to have more stamina than her opponent and fought back to win, 6–4.

But her comeback came with a cost. In the hot weather, working hard, Venus began to cramp up in the third set. That's the only advantage Hingis needed. As she said later, "I tried to keep her running. I knew she was cramping up."

Hingis drew away in the middle of the set, and Venus was powerless to keep up. The early rounds had taken a toll on her stamina. She lost, 6–3. There would be no all-Williams final, and perhaps no Grand Slam win for a Williams in the tournament.

But Venus knew her tough match with Hingis may have helped tire out her sister's opponent. "Now Serena's playing for two people. I gave Martina a good workout today." Hingis would have only one day to rest. The final was scheduled for the following day.

When the two young women took the court, it soon became clear that Venus was correct. Hingis looked drawn and tired. In contrast, Serena looked quick and strong.

In the first set, Serena overwhelmed her opponent, running her all over the court and reaching every return Hingis made. She cruised to a 6–3 first-set win.

But Hingis, despite being only eighteen years old, was a veteran of many tennis wars. She sensed that her own game was off and abandoned her attacking game. Instead, she played strategically, just keeping the ball in play, hoping for Serena to make some mistakes.

The strategy worked. In the second set, Serena

began to tire and made some unforced errors. Hingis knew that if she could just get the match to a third set she'd out-last her opponent.

Nevertheless, Serena took a 5–3 lead. She needed only one more game to win the tournament.

But Hingis didn't give in. She stuck to her plan and hoped that Serena would be too anxious to win and make some mistakes.

The two battled to match point, but Hingis fought Serena off to take the game and make it 5–4. Then Serena took her to match point a second time. Once more Hingis calmly fought her off. The two battled to 6–6. The match would go to a tiebreaker.

The pressure was on Serena. If she lost, she was almost certain to suffer a letdown in the third set. Hingis would have a good chance to come back and win.

Serena didn't want the match to go to a third set. She wanted to win now.

It was Serena who received a second wind. Her strength returned, and she used her serve and a series of powerful ground strokes to inch ahead. With the score 6–4 in the tiebreaker, she stood getting ready to serve, knowing that if she won this point the

U.S. Open championship — a Grand Slam title — would be hers.

She took a quick glance in the stands and drew a deep breath. It was as if her entire tennis career had come down to one shot. Thousands of hours of practice were distilled into a single moment.

She bounced the ball on the ground several times, then held it before her in her left hand, her racket in her right hand hanging at her side. The stands were absolutely quiet. Then she tossed the ball into the air and exploded, hoping for an ace.

Thwack! The serve boomed across the net.

Hingis reacted quickly to the powerful serve, defensively fighting it off. She managed to hit the ball, but not quite the way she intended. The ball struck her racket just off center. And instead of striking the ball with her racket perpendicular to the ground, it was tilted slightly back. Her return was weak, looping into the air.

Serena tracked the ball with her eyes and followed it across the court. She sensed that it would be long, but as if she refused to believe it, she jogged back after the ball. As one sportswriter noted, she was "holding her racket in front of her like a shovel, ready to pounce if anything went wrong," ready to return the ball just in case it took a sudden dip and landed in.

It didn't. The referee calmly called, "Out."

Serena had won! She was the U.S. Open champion. She had won a Grand Slam title!

Her knees buckled and she dropped to the ground, a look of utter surprise on her face as the crowd erupted in cheers. She held her quivering hands to her face and began screaming, "Oh my God! Oh my God!" She looked around the stadium in disbelief as everyone stood and applauded. That included her sister Venus and most of the Williams family.

In a daze, she congratulated Hingis and stepped to one side of the court for the trophy presentation, basking in the applause as an engraver quickly added the name "Serena Williams" to the list of former champions like Althea Gibson, Chris Evert, and Martina Navratilova. When she received the trophy she looked at it closely. "That's my name right there," she said.

A few moments later, a tennis official handed her a phone. President Clinton called to offer his congratulations. Serena was in a daze. When he asked her how she felt, she blurted out. "I'm pretty stoked!"

So was the rest of the tennis world.

Chapter Nine:
1999–2000

Venus Rising

Serena was on a roll. Just a month after winning the U.S. Open, she defeated Venus for the first time, beating her in three sets to win a title in Munich, Germany. "I was cruising today," she said afterward. "I'd never actually beaten Venus. I don't know how it feels."

Venus did. Although she tried to put her defeat into perspective, saying, "It's a win-win situation. One daughter is going to win. What's the difference?" the loss served as a wake-up call. As much as the sisters tried to deflect attention from their emerging rivalry, neither young woman liked to lose. Venus entered the 2000 season determined to make amends.

More than anything else, Venus hoped to capture

her first Grand Slam title. She knew that until she did that, she would never be considered a truly great player.

Serena and Venus got off to slow starts in 2000, as each was hampered by tendonitis in the knee. For a while, there were even rumors that Venus would retire. But as spring turned to summer, both sisters recovered and began to play better tennis. Because of the injuries, they had missed out on a chance to win a Grand Slam title in either the Australian or the French Opens. Both looked forward to Wimbledon in July, hoping to capture that elusive title.

When Venus was a young girl, she dreamed of one day winning Wimbledon, the most prestigious and storied Grand Slam title. Her only problem was that Serena shared the same dream.

Venus was seeded fifth in the tournament, while Serena was seeded eighth. The tournament draw set up a potential semifinal meeting between the two.

Both Venus and Serena set their sights on the title and played well in the early rounds. To no one's surprise, they each reached the semifinals.

Their match was one of the most anticipated

events in Wimbledon history. The winner would face Lindsay Davenport in the final.

But once again, the matchup was a critical disappointment. With so much at stake, the sisters seemed to have a hard time playing very well against each other. Richard Williams couldn't even bear to watch. He walked the streets around the All England Club while his two daughters battled it out.

Serena was off her game from the very beginning. Venus played steady if unspectacular tennis and won the first set easily, 6–2.

Serena fought back in the second set, which went to a tiebreaker. Then her serve deserted her. On match point she double-faulted. As her final serve plunked into the net, she blinked back tears as Venus walked over to her, put her arm around her, and slowly escorted her off the court.

Serena was crushed, not so much because she lost to her sister, but because she knew she hadn't played very well. "I expected to play a lot better," she said. "It was my goal to do better."

Venus seemed to take little joy from the win. "It's not really so much fun. If it was a final it would be different, but it was a semifinal and I hated to see Serena go."

Then someone asked her how she felt about playing for the championship. She perked up. "Hopefully it'll be the U.S. Open and I'll follow through and rebound for the Williamses," she said. If she did, she'd become the first African-American women's champion since Althea Gibson in 1958.

"This has always been my dream. Sometimes I'd dream I'd win Grand Slams and I'd wake up and it's just terrible because I haven't."

She knew that it would be difficult to beat Lindsay Davenport. The defending Wimbledon champion held a 9–3 advantage in twelve previous meetings with Venus. Moreover, it would be the first time the two met on a grass surface.

"That's going to change the whole dimension of the match," said Davenport. "Venus has been playing really well and I know I'm going to have to play my best to win."

Venus took center court knowing that she had to control the match from the beginning. When Davenport was able to get a lead, she played with a great deal of confidence. She was very difficult to come back against.

When Venus started the match, she played nervous tennis. She made three unforced errors and lost her serve in the first game.

Then she settled down, winning four straight games to take control. She won the first set, 6–3.

Davenport quickly recovered to take a 2–0 lead in the second set. She'd seemed to settle into a nice rhythm, staying behind the baseline and patiently returning Venus's booming shots. Venus knew she needed a break before Davenport got on a roll and pushed the match to a third set.

She got one. All of a sudden Davenport's normally accurate serve deserted her. She double-faulted Venus back into the match. Venus fought hard to take a 5–4 lead. Victory was close enough to touch.

But Venus suddenly seemed overwhelmed. Now she had a hard time getting *her* serve in. Before she knew it, the match was tied and forced into a tiebreaker. As she said later, "I wanted to hit the ball before it could even get over the net, which isn't good because you rush."

Once the tiebreaker began, Venus seemed to relax and jumped out to a 6–3 lead. Then it was her turn to stand at service, needing only one more point for victory.

She reminded herself not to rush. She'd already double-faulted her way out of one match point, and she was determined not to let it happen again.

She boomed a serve to Davenport's forehand. Davenport stretched out and sent a return hurtling back.

It was into the net! Venus had won!

"Oh, my!" she yelled out. Then she dashed to the net, shook hands with Davenport, and ran into the stands. She gave Serena a long hug. Her sister started crying, this time with tears of joy. Then Venus hugged her father. He'd been beside himself all day, waving a sign that said, "It's Venus's party and no one is invited." Indeed it was.

At the press conference after the match, Venus couldn't contain her excitement. "I love Wimbledon. I love playing tennis. I love winning titles," she babbled. "This was meant to be."

Now that she had the elusive Grand Slam victory

and was feeling healthy, Venus was relaxed. She responded by playing some of the best tennis of her career.

Tennis fans could hardly wait for the U.S. Open in September. It seemed almost certain that the Williams sisters would meet in the finals. Serena would be looking to defend her title, and Venus would be hoping to win a second consecutive Grand Slam title. In recent months, the sisters had been almost unbeatable.

But Serena received a tough draw in the tournament. She faced Lindsay Davenport in the quarterfinals and was eliminated.

That opened the door for Venus. But even as she readied herself, a shadow fell over the tournament. Reports that Davenport and Hingis had made a promise to one another to do whatever they could to prevent an all-Williams final started to circulate. When asked, Davenport admitted that it was true. "Martina and I had a little talk — we didn't want that to happen."

Some observers criticized Davenport for her remarks. After all, the U.S. Open was an American tournament and it didn't seem right for her to root against another American.

Although the Williams sisters were much more popular with other tour members than they had once been, there was still some resentment over their success and unorthodox style. Some players whispered that Richard Williams decided which daughter would win when the two faced each other, and that they sometimes worked as a team in tournaments, extending matches to wear down certain opponents for the benefit of the other.

The sisters dismissed such reports as sour grapes. They were sisters first, and knew that nothing they ever did would prevent people from seeing them that way. After all, that's what they were.

Davenport had already done her part to keep a Williams out of the finals. She dumped Elena Dementieva in the semis to advance to the finals. Meanwhile, Venus faced Hingis in the other semifinal.

The two played a tough three-set match that Venus won. The finals of the U.S. Open would reprise the finals at Wimbledon and be the first all-American women's finals at the Open in more than twenty years. Davenport was looking for revenge, and Venus was hoping to avenge her sister's loss.

Both players were at the top of their game. Davenport had won twenty-one straight matches on the women's tour. Witnesses later described the match as the hardest-hitting final in the history of women's tennis. The two squared off like boxers throwing haymakers and blasted the ball back and forth the entire match.

Venus took center court wearing a delicate tiara in her hair. Earlier that year both Venus and Serena had abandoned their signature beads-and-braids look. They were women now.

Each woman tried the same approach, staying back and blasting line-drive returns aimed at the corners. At first, Davenport was the more successful, as more of her shots found the corner than did Venus's. She jumped out to a commanding 4–1 lead.

But Venus still had one advantage over Davenport — her serve. Blasting the ball at nearly 120 miles per hour, she fought back. She finally broke Davenport's serve and won five straight games. Davenport ended the first set in horrible fashion, double-faulting twice in a row. As her final serve went awry and delivered the set to Venus, 6–4, she grimaced and noticeably sagged. "I should have won that set," she said later.

There was no stopping Venus. This time there would be no letdown.

The two players slugged it out, but Venus proved again and again that she wasn't only the stronger of the two, she was also faster. Over and over, she stretched out and made almost-impossible returns, not just getting to the ball, but getting to it and making a great shot of her own. After nearly two hours of play, she came away with her second consecutive Grand Slam win when she took the second set, 7–5.

Venus was more restrained after this victory than at Wimbledon, but not by much. She did a twirl and skipped to the net to shake hands with her opponent before reaching into the crowd, where this time her mother received the first hug.

"It feels really nice," she said of the win, which earned a telephone call of her own from President Clinton. "It was a nice victory, because I feel like I played Lindsay at her best." Even Davenport had to admit that. "Venus was playing great," she said. "She forced me to play better."

Venus had precious little time to enjoy her win. Just a few weeks later she traveled to Sydney, Australia, for the 2000 Olympics. She had been named a member of the American women's team, one of two players, along with Davenport, competing in singles. Serena made the team as well, paired with Venus in doubles competition.

Since each country can send only a few players to the Olympics, the tennis competition was a notch below that of the WTA tour and lacked the prestige of a Grand Slam event. Still, it was the Olympics, and the Williams sisters looked forward to representing their country and meeting the other athletes from around the world at the Olympic Village.

What made it even nicer was the opportunity to work with U.S. team coach Billie Jean King and her assistant, Zina Garrison. Both Venus and Serena loved the opportunity to work with the two former champions.

In singles competition, Lindsay Davenport was forced to withdraw after the first round with a foot injury. That put the pressure on Venus. She was a heavy favorite to win a gold medal.

She played like a champion, easily making her

way to the finals. Assured of no less than a silver medal, she faced Russia's Elena Dementieva for the gold.

It was no contest. Displaying a newfound maturity, Venus easily dispatched her Russian opponent, 6–2, 6–2. She was humbled by the opportunity to represent her country and relished the win.

"This is one moment in time for me, for my country, for my family, for the team," she said. "I felt really excited. I watched the Olympics at home when I was a kid, and it was one of my dreams to win an Olympic medal. It means a lot."

Now that she had one gold medal, it was time to go for another. Venus and Serena had won 22 consecutive doubles matches. They didn't plan on losing now.

King and Garrison worked them hard, impressing upon the sisters the necessity of teamwork. Even though they were on a big winning streak, they tended to overpower their opponents with their individual skill. King and Garrison wanted them to learn to work together more.

The young women took that lesson to heart. In one of the most dominating performances in Olympic history, they crushed the opposition, losing only one set on their way to the finals. All that stood in the way of a gold medal was the Dutch team of Kristie Boogert and Miriam Oremans.

All the years of practice, from the public courts of Compton to center court at the Grand Slams, came together for the sisters. They obliterated the two Dutch women, 6–1, 6–1. Now each sister had a gold medal.

It had been a great year for Venus, and with the gold medal in the Olympics, a great year for Serena as well. From the looks of things, there would be many more great years ahead.

Chapter Ten:
2001

Onward and Upward?

As Venus and Serena Williams continue their careers, there seems to be no limit to what they can achieve. Each has been in the spotlight for so long it is easy to forget that they are still quite young. Their best years could still be ahead of them.

On the court, there is much left for them to do. Neither seems satisfied with just one or two Grand Slam titles, and each sister has said that she one day hopes to be ranked number one in their sport, a ranking that has thus far eluded them. They have plenty of motivation, not only from each other and from the other players on the WTA tour, but from history. No one can yet predict just how good they

become.

both Serena and Venus have demon-

are stars in their sports,

their feet are securely on the ground. In between rounds of tennis, each young woman takes college classes, and they have both begun to speak of a time when tennis is no longer the center of their lives. Each has thrown her support to a variety of charitable causes and gone out of her way to speak to young people and give tennis clinics, particularly in the African-American community. Richard Williams continues to drop hints that his daughters might soon decide to retire from the sport. He appears to have fulfilled his goal of teaching his youngest daughters that there is much more to the world than the tennis court.

Both are well on their way to speaking four foreign languages — French, Italian, German, and Russian. Each has studied fashion design and begun to design her own clothing. Venus surfs and loves to collect antique furniture, while Serena prefers a skateboard and plays guitar. If their tennis careers were to come to a sudden end, one has the feeling that each young woman would quickly find something else to fulfill her life.

As the sisters have grown and matured, they have become more independent. They've beg beyond the close-knit confines of their extended family. Venus and Serena live away from their parents now, in a home they share, and they have begun to explore the variety of options that their success has made available to them. The sisters have written and published their own tennis newsletter and have flirted with Hollywood, taking screen tests for possible entertainment careers. But most importantly, both Venus and Serena have remained themselves.

Although their relationship with their father remains controversial at times, Venus and Serena continue to display remarkable self-assurance and confidence. Perhaps more than any title either young woman has won, what is most impressive about them is that each has avoided the pitfalls that come with success, particularly at such a young age. They remain happily and gloriously themselves, but they know that everyone is paying attention all the time.

"We definitely have a large impact," said Venus once. "People are watching what Serena and I do. I guess they want to be a part of it."

thing is certain. In the next few years, it will
d see what Venus and Serena will

Matt Christopher

Kobe Bryant

Terrell Davis

Julie Foudy

Jeff Gordon

Wayne Gretzky

Ken Griffey Jr.

Mia Hamm

Tony Hawk

Grant Hill

Derek Jeter

Randy Johnson

Michael Jordan

Tara Lipinski

Mark McGwire

Greg Maddux

Hakeem Olajuwon

Alex Rodriguez

Briana Scurry

Sammy Sosa

Venus and
Serena Williams

Tiger Woods

Steve Young

The #1
Sports Series
for Kids

Read them all!

Baseball Pals

Baseball Turnaround

The Basket Counts

Catch That Pass!

Catcher with a Glass Arm

Center Court Sting

Challenge at Second Base

The Comeback Challenge

Cool as Ice

The Counterfeit Tackle

Crackerjack Halfback

Diamond Champs

Dive Right ...

Double Play at Short

Face-Off

Football Fugitive

Football Nightmare

The Fox Steals Home

The Great Quarterback Switch

The Hockey Machine

Ice Magic

Inline Skater

Johnny Long Legs

The Kid Who Only Hit Homers

Long-Arm Quarterback

Long Shot for Paul

Who's Playing First Base

Plate

Mountain Bike Mania

No Arm in Left Field

Olympic Dream

Penalty Shot

Pressure Play

Prime-Time Pitcher

Red-Hot Hightops

The Reluctant Pitcher

Return of the Home Run Kid

Roller Hockey Radicals

Run, Billy, Run

Shoot for the Hoop

Shortstop from Tokyo

Skateboard Renegade

Skateboard Tough

Snowboard Maverick

Snowboard Showdown

Soccer Duel

Soccer Halfback

Soccer Scoop

Spike It!

The Submarine Pitch

Supercharged Infield

The Team That Couldn't Lose

Tennis Ace

Tight End

Too Hot to Handle

Top Wing

Touchdown for Tommy

Tough to Tackle

Wheel Wizards

Windmill Windup

Wingman on Ice

The Year Mom Won the Pennant

All available in paperback fro